D0650647

Peace

Peace

by
Joyce Meyer

Harrison House
Tulsa, Oklahoma

Unless otherwise indicated, all Scripture quotations are taken from the *King James Version* of the Bible.

Scripture quotations marked AMP are taken from *The Amplified Bible, Old Testament* copyright © 1965, 1987 by Zondervan Corporation. *New Testament* copyright © 1958, 1987 by the Lockman Foundation. Used by Permission.

Scripture quotations marked NKJV are taken from *The New King James Version* of the Bible. Copyright ©1979, 1980, 1982, 1983, 1984 by Thomas Nelson, Inc. Publishers. Used by permission.

7th Printing

Peace
ISBN 0-89274-922-9
Copyright © 1995 by Joyce Meyer
Life In The Word, Inc.
P. O. Box 655
Fenton, Missouri 63026

Published by Harrison House, Inc.
P. O. Box 35035
Tulsa, Oklahoma 74153

Printed in the United States of America. All rights reserved under International Copyright Law. Contents and/or cover may not be reproduced in whole or in part in any form without the expressed written consent of the Publisher.

Contents

Foreword

"...search for peace (harmony; undisturbedness from fears, agitating passions, and moral conflicts) and seek it eagerly. [Do not merely desire peaceful relations with God, with your fellowmen, and with yourself, but pursue, go after them!]"

1 Peter 3:11 AMP

I pray this book on peace will help you learn to enjoy "...the peace of God, which passeth all understanding..." (Phil. 4:7).

Are You Enjoying Peace?

1

....

Are You Enjoying Peace?

Every born-again child of God should be enjoying a life full of peace. Jesus said in John 14:27 (AMP):

"Peace I leave with you; My [own] peace I now give and bequeath to you. Not as the world gives do I give to you. Do not let your hearts be troubled, neither let them be afraid. [Stop allowing yourselves to be agitated and disturbed; and do not permit yourselves to be fearful and intimidated and cowardly and unsettled.]"

This is really a powerful Scripture. Please read it several times, then take at least five minutes to meditate on it and let it soak in.

First, let us notice that the peace Jesus offers is a special peace, not like the world gives. What kind of peace does the world offer? The world offers a certain *feeling* of peace. This peace operates when everything in your life is going the way you want it to. However, when things are not going your way, that worldly peace flees in a big hurry. The spirit of "upset" quickly takes over. The peace Jesus gives operates in good times or bad, when you are abounding or being abased. His peace operates in the middle of the storm.

It would be wonderful, as far as the carnal mind is concerned, if everything went your way all the time. We know by experience that in real life this does not happen. As a believer, I tried for years to use my faith to remove anything and everything I did not like or that did not feel good. This caused me tremendous frustration. Trying to make something happen that cannot and will not happen is always very frustrating. After getting some experience with God, I finally began to realize that I needed to use my faith to calmly and peacefully go through the storms and trials of life. I needed to stop allowing the devil to steal my peace every time I turned around.

Jesus said in John 14:27 (AMP), "Stop allowing yourselves to be agitated and disturbed." The more I read this Scripture and pondered it, the more I realized the Bible was telling me that I was doing it to myself. I needed to stop it. He also said in that verse, "Do not let not your hearts be troubled, neither let them be afraid."

Jesus rebuked the disciples in Mark 4:40 for a lack of faith because they lost their peace in the storm. Jesus did not lose His peace. He was asleep in the back of the boat. The disciples were in a panic and very much upset.

What about you? Would you have been in the back of the boat enjoying peace with Jesus? *If you do not have peace, you are not enjoying life.*

How To Enjoy Peace

2

....

How To Enjoy Peace

No message is very helpful unless some instruction is given on "how to" obtain the thing you need. To say you need peace is step one. However, without practically sharing how you can have peace, no real fruit is borne.

One thing helped me tremendously to begin to enjoy a peaceful life. I realized it was useless and extremely frustrating to "try to do something about something I could not do anything about." Are you doing that? Are you frustrating yourself trying to make things happen? God has a perfect timing for everything. You must wait on His timing.

Generally, you cannot make things happen out of their season anyway. Even if you did birth something out of season, you would never be happy with it. Learn to wait on God. This brings Him honor, and it brings you peace.

Are you trying to do the impossible? Are you trying to change the people around you – perhaps the person you are married to, one of your children, a friend, or a relative? People cannot change people. Only God can get inside a person's heart and cause him or her to want to change. If we force people from the outside by making demands on them, it ends up stealing everyone's peace. We are not created to be put under the law. People need freedom. They need space to move in.

I tried to force Dave to stop playing golf the first several years of our marriage. I felt he played too much, and I wanted to be with him more. I tried every way I could. I used every trick. I pouted. I got mad. I tried to convince him. I gave him the silent treatment. Nothing worked. I was upset all the time. Once in a while, he would give up and not play for a while. The interesting thing was that even though I got what I wanted, I still did not have peace. I did not have peace because I tried to get what I wanted the wrong way. If you are trying to force someone to change, it will steal your peace.

Are you upset with yourself a lot because you are not where you would like to be spiritually? Are you trying to change yourself? You certainly need to cooperate with the Holy Spirit concerning the work He is doing in your life. He is bringing you into perfection or maturity. You cannot do it yourself. This is another area of trying to do something you cannot do.

I am sure you can see it is a very natural thing to try to make things change that you do not like. Be realistic for a moment. How successful are you being at changing these things? Are you simply frustrating yourself and losing your peace when you should be resting in God, waiting on Him and His timing, trusting Him with the other people in your life and even with your own self?

Let me sum it up by saying this: if you are "trying to do something about something you cannot do anything about," you will be frustrated and will not enjoy peace.

Be Led by Peace

3

Be Led by Peace

Colossians 3:15 (AMP) says:

"And let the peace (soul harmony which comes) from Christ rule (act as umpire continually) in your hearts [deciding and settling with finality all questions that arise in your minds...]."

The umpire in a ball game decides if you are in or out. Peace is to be the umpire that decides if a thing should be in your life or out.

Many people do not enjoy peace because they are out of the will of God. They follow their own will rather than God's will. They do what they feel like or what they think is right rather than following God's Word and being led by peace. Quite often something comes up that I want to do. It sounds good, feels good, and can even be a good thing. However, if I do not have peace, I have learned to leave it alone. *Be led by peace*. Do not buy something, especially a major purchase, if you do not have peace about it. No matter how much you want it, you will be sorry if you go against the leading of the Holy Spirit.

Occasionally I will be offered an opportunity for a speaking engagement that I would like to take, but I do not have peace about it. I do not know why, but sometimes the peace is just not there. I have learned that if I take it anyway, a reason always turns up regarding why I should have followed peace.

One engagement I remember was when I first started traveling. Speaking engagements were very few and far between. Naturally, I wanted to take them all. I received an invitation to a church in Texas. That was really exciting for me at the time. I said "yes" right away. A couple of weeks later, I got this gnawing on my insides every time I thought about it. It got stronger and stronger. I just plainly had no peace about going, and yet God gave me no reason why.

I waited and waited. Finally, I knew I had to call them and ask for a release from the commitment. I told them I would come if they could not find a suitable replacement, but for some reason, I had no peace about going. They did release me from the commitment.

A few weeks later I found out that my home church was dedicating their new building the weekend I would have been gone. I had been an associate pastor in that church for quite some time before starting my own ministry, and it was very important for me to be with them on that occasion.

Why didn't the Lord just tell me what was going on? For some reason, He chose not to. His Word says to be led by peace. Many times that is all He will give you to let you know if you are "in" or "out" of His will. Later you may know why, or you may never know why.

You will never enjoy a peaceful life if you disobey His leading and follow your own will.

What Are Your Peace Stealers?

4

....

What Are Your
Peace Stealers?

Certain things bother each individual. Satan has spent all of your life studying you. He probably knows you better than you know yourself. He knows what bothers you. *You need to know what bothers you,* and be careful in those times not to lose your peace.

Everyone's "peace stealers" are not the same. There are things that bother me that do not bother Dave at all. For example, I like quiet, but noise does not bother him. He can read a book while one of our daughters has her tape recorder turned on full blast and our nine-year-old son wrestles on the floor with the dog.

I cannot stand to hurry, and I hate to be late. Sometimes Dave will try to do too much in an allotted time. We will end up at the last minute in a big hurry. This is something the devil knows about me, and he will use it to try to steal my peace. Dave, on the other hand, always wants to get to the airport at least an hour early when we fly anywhere. He always wants to get to the golf course early when he is going to play golf. If the devil can arrange for him to be late for one of those events, Dave begins to lose his peace.

We are different. Therefore, Satan uses different tactics with each of us. Be smarter than he is. *He sets you up to get you upset.* What are your "peace stealers"? Make a list and discuss them with your family. Find out what really irritates them, then try to help each other avoid those areas.

Dave is a serious golfer. I play, but it would suit me just fine to laugh and giggle my way around the course. I have learned, however, that it is not wise for me to goof around a lot when I am playing golf with Dave or to tease him when he hits a bad shot. We have fun, but I need to do what is comfortable for him. There is no sense in driving someone else to lose his or her peace. When you live with someone a long time, you begin to know his or her weaknesses as well as your own. I repeat, "Try to help each other avoid those areas."

Dave helps me in my weaknesses. He tries to help keep things quiet when I am trying to study or rest. He encourages me to get rest and recreation because he knows if I get too tired, Satan will steal my peace. Galatians 6:2 (NKJV) says, "Bear one another's burdens...." We need to bear each other's weaknesses, realize we all have plenty of them and pray for one another.

Why Does the
Devil Try To Steal
Your Peace?

5

Why Does the Devil Try To Steal Your Peace?

We know that peace binds us to the Holy Spirit. Another way to say it is that the Holy Spirit works only in an atmosphere of peace. *There is power in peace.* I believe that is why John 14:27 (AMP) tells us that our legacy from Jesus is peace. Jesus said, "...My [own] peace I now give and bequeath to you...." In other words, He wills His peace to us.

If you have a problem and the devil cannot drive you to be upset about it, he has no power over you. Your power is in maintaining a calm, peaceful, trusting attitude. The devil's power is in causing you to be upset and fearful.

When you find yourself in a troublesome situation, let your goal be to simply stay calm. Do not play into the devil's hands by getting upset. He delights in getting you emotionally upset. Usually, the first thing a person does when he is in an emotional state is say things out of his mouth that give the devil fuel to add to the fire he has just started.

James 3:5,6 (paraphrased) says the tongue is a little member, but it can start a big fire. It is a world of wickedness set among our members contaminating and depraving the whole body, and it is a fire ignited by hell. You can see from this Scripture that the devil wants you to lose control so that he can gain control. Remember, *the devil sets you up to get you upset.*

You may have noticed that the devil will work overtime when you are getting ready to go to church or to a Bible study. For years, Sunday morning around our house seemed like a big blowout. We rarely made it to church without someone getting upset, and usually it was everyone.

On Sunday morning, things would get lost, spilled and broken like no other day of the week. Our children could get along well every other day of the week, but on Sunday morning, they would fight. The more noise and commotion we had, the more upset I became. (Remember, I do not like a lot of noise.)

Finally, I would start complaining. Dave hates complaining, so after a while, he would tell me to stop complaining. Then I would get mad at him. Then the children would cry because Dave and I were arguing.

In the middle of all this, the dog would start running around the house with the shoe somebody needed to wear, then I would start hollering, "Hurry up! We're going to be late!" I am sure you recognize the scene.

When I saw James 3:18, I understood why this seemed to always happen when we were going out to hear the Word. This Scripture says (AMP), "the harvest of righteousness..." (right actions) "...is [the fruit of the seed] sown" (the Word) "in peace by those who work for and make peace."

In other words, in order for the Word of God to take root and produce good fruit in our lives, it must be preached or taught by someone who is a peacemaker himself. Also, we need to be in a peaceful attitude when we hear the Word.

Just think about your own life. How many times is the enemy successful in his attempt to get you upset before you go to hear the Word? Remember to watch for his scheme, then do not play into his hands. Second Corinthians 2:11 (AMP) says that "we are not ignorant" of Satan's "wiles and intentions." The *King James Version* calls them "devices." Satan uses his wiles to deceive and lead astray. Let's be smarter than the devil.

First Peter 5:8 (AMP) says: "Be well balanced (temperate, sober of mind), be vigilant and cautious at all times; for that enemy of yours, the devil, roams around like a lion roaring [in fierce hunger], seeking someone to seize upon and devour."

Do not let it be you! I exhort you to be cautious. Each time you begin to feel upset or frustrated, stop and ask yourself these questions: "What is the devil trying to do? If I give place to these negative emotions, what will the result be?"

Ephesians 4:26,27 (AMP) are also very important Scriptures that teach us to keep the devil from getting a foothold in our lives by not being upset. Verse 26 says, "...do not ever let your wrath (your exasperation, your fury or indignation) last until the sun goes down." In other words, "Don't stay upset."

Verse 27 (AMP) says, "Leave no [such] room or foothold for the devil [give no opportunity to him]." When you are upset, you lose your joy. When you lose your joy, you lose your strength. Nehemiah 8:10 says, "...the joy of the Lord is your strength." The psalmist, David, in Psalm 42:5 (NKJV) speaks to his own soul and says, "Why are you... disquieted within me?..." Isaiah 30:15 says, "...in quietness and in confidence shall be your strength...." We see once again that the devil wants to disquiet us in order to steal our strength.

I learned from the Holy Spirit that He works in an atmosphere of peace. The Holy Spirit does not work in turmoil. The devil works in turmoil, but the Holy Spirit works in peace. Provide a peaceful atmosphere in your home, business, church or ministry. As you do so, you will be honoring the Word of God and the Spirit of God. You will reap the fruit of your obedience.

Remember, Jesus sent the seventy out two by two to do many mighty works: to cast out devils, heal the sick and preach the Gospel. He told them to go into a town, find a house, speak peace to it and remain there. If they were not received (peacefully), they were to shake the dust off their feet and move on. (Luke 10:1-11,17.) Why? Their work would be powerless unless they dwelt in peace.

I am sure you are beginning to get a revelation on the message this book intends to bring forth. *Do your utmost to exercise self-control to remain in peace always.*

In Luke 22:46, Jesus teaches us to pray that we come not into temptation. He said to the disciples (AMP), "...Get up and pray that you may not enter [at all] into temptation." Do not rely on yourself or your strength to resist the devil in this area. Pray daily that God will give you grace to resist the devil when he tries to steal your peace. Ask the Lord to strengthen you and to help you.

Remember, John 15:5 (AMP) says, "apart from Me...you can do nothing." Do not try to do it by yourself! Ask for help. You can do all things through Christ (Phil. 4:13) but nothing by yourself. In John 5:30 (AMP), even Jesus said He could do nothing from Himself. You must have a humble attitude if you want God to help you. First Peter 5:5 (NKJV) says, "...God resists the proud, but gives grace to the humble."

Let me summarize by saying that Satan wants to steal your peace so that he can steal your strength. He wants you weak and powerless, but I encourage you to "...be strong in the Lord, and in the power of his might" (Eph. 6:10). *Remain in peace!*

The Believer's
Position
During Trials

6

....

The Believer's Position During Trials

Ephesians 6:13 (AMP) says, "...having done all [the crisis demands], to stand [firmly in your place]." What is "your place"? Ephesians 2:6 teaches us that our place is *in Christ*. The word *stand* is a translation from the Greek word *histemi*.[1] One of the meanings is "abide." The Greek word for *abide* in John 15:7 is *meno*. One of the meanings is "stand."[2] *Meno* is sometimes translated as *stand*.[3] Jesus said, "If you abide in Me, and My words abide in you, you will ask what you desire, and it shall be done for you" (John 15:7 NKJV). The abiding position is a place of power.

---

[1] James Strong, "Greek Dictionary of the New Testament," *Strong's Exhaustive Concordance of the Bible*, (Abingdon: Nashville, 1890), p. 38, entry #2476.

[2] Strong, *Concordance*, "Greek," p. 47, #3306.

[3] W. E. Vine, *An Expository Dictionary of New Testament Words* (Old Tappan: Fleming H. Revell, 1940), Vol. IV, pp. 70, 71.

Hebrews 4 says that when you cease your struggles, laboring instead (through faith and obedience) to enter the rest of God, you *will* enter His rest. In a time of trial, do what God leads you to do, then abide or take your position *in Christ* and watch Him work in your behalf. The Bible says, "...stand still, and see the salvation of the Lord" (Ex. 14:13). All of these words – abide, still, rest, stand, and in Christ – say the same basic thing: *Do not lose your peace!*

Philippians 1:28 (AMP) is one of the most powerful Scriptures in the Bible that brings this point across loud and clear. It says:

"And do not [for a moment] be frightened or intimidated in anything by your opponents and adversaries, for such [constancy and fearlessness] will be a clear sign (proof and seal) to them of [their impending] destruction, but [a sure token and evidence] of your deliverance and salvation, and that from God."

This Scripture plainly lays it out. *When you are attacked, stay in peace.*

That tells the devil he is defeated. He does not know what to do with you if he cannot get you upset. It also assures you of being delivered by God because this attitude of peace and rest shows God you are operating in real faith. Hebrews 4 says that those who enter the rest of God have believed.

Go ahead and enjoy your life while God works on your problems. I believe most people have a vague type of thinking that says it is wrong to enjoy yourself when you have problems. After all, if you cannot do anything else, you can at least be miserable.

I know I experienced a lot of this type of thinking in past years. When Dave and I would have some sort of trial or problem, he would be happy and enjoy himself. I would be miserable and mad at him because he would not be miserable with me.

Often our struggle would be financial. Dave seemed to have a supernatural faith in the area of money. He would say, "We tithe and give generous offerings as we see needs. The Bible says, "Casting all your care upon him; for he careth for you" (1 Pet. 5:7). The Bible says, God will meet our needs (Phil. 4:19), so why should I worry about it? Worrying will not bring the money in. It never does."

This was the "stand" Dave took. While God was working on the problem, Dave went ahead and enjoyed his life. I said, "I know all that, Dave, but you cannot just do nothing." I wanted him to do something. He would say, "Okay, Joyce, what do you want me to do?" I would say, "Pray! You should pray." He would say, "I did. I prayed and asked God to take care of the problem. I asked Him to show me if there was anything else He wanted me to do. He hasn't shown me anything, so I don't see any point in being miserable."

I knew deep down inside Dave was right. Still, there was a vague something that kept insisting I should not have the audacity to enjoy myself while I had a problem. The outcome was the same for years: every time we had a problem Dave would pray and stay in peace, and I would pray and worry. I made myself miserable. Dave enjoyed his life, and God always came through in the end. We always made it.

Thank God, I finally realized I was not accomplishing anything. All that I was doing was making myself miserable and probably prolonging the answer God wanted to give. Now I enjoy *peace in the midst of the storm.* (Mark 4:37-40.)

Jesus said, "In the world you will have tribulation; but be of good cheer, I have overcome the world" (John 16:33b NKJV). The Bible also says temptation must come, but we are exhorted not to get into the temptation. (Luke 8:13; 1 Cor. 10:13; James 1:12.) My point is that challenges, things to overcome, will always be there in this life, but we are overcomers through Christ Jesus. (Rom. 8:37.)

We are not *overcamers,* but we are always *overcomers.* You will never reach a place where you have already overcome every obstacle, but you can have the assurance of always triumphing in Christ. You are always overcoming!

You will have to come to the place Paul talked about in Philippians 4:11,12 – he said he learned to be content (peaceful) whether he was being abased or abounding. If you do not, your life will consist of one series of upsets after another. Remember this: If the devil can control you with circumstances, he will have you under his thumb all the time. You can walk in your authority by always being in peace.

One Day at a Time

7

....

One Day at a Time

A sure way to lose your peace is to start worrying about tomorrow. Matthew 6:34 (AMP) says:

"So do not worry or be anxious about tomorrow, for tomorrow will have worries and anxieties of its own. Sufficient for each day is its own trouble."

Most of us have enough to handle today without worrying about tomorrow. God will give you grace for today, but He will not give you grace for tomorrow until tomorrow arrives.

So often people worry and worry about something that never happens. The "what ifs" are trouble. When you hear "what if" this or that going through your mind, be careful. You are probably about to be dragged off into worry. Some people worry so much that their worries become fear, and often the things people fear come to them. We can receive from God through faith. We can also receive from the devil through fear.

Do not allow yourself to dread tomorrow. Just know that God is faithful. *Whatever tomorrow holds, He holds tomorrow.* His grace is sufficient to meet the need. Do not waste today's grace to enjoy today by worrying about tomorrow. It is absolutely amazing what we can accomplish in Christ if we live one day at a time.

I learned this lesson when I started teaching Bible college. I was teaching once a week at my home church where I was also Associate Pastor. I had four children and a full-time job already when the opportunity came to teach Bible college at the church three times each week. I had a real desire to teach the Word more, and here was an opportunity to teach three times each week.

However, when I teach, I also have to study and prepare. A lot of the classes would be in-depth Bible study, which would mean a lot of digging in the Word for me to get ready, especially the first year. All of the studying had to be done in the evenings, because my job was during the day. I did not see how I could possibly do it, but I felt God wanted me to.

After much prayer and thought, I stepped out in God to do the impossible in Him. The main thing the Lord kept impressing on me was: "One day at a time, and you can do it." If I started thinking about tomorrow, I would get in trouble really fast because immediately I would see the impossibility. Yet, each day, one day at a time, it all worked out. God gave me grace, but not until the day I needed it. The second year was a lot easier because I had all my lessons. Therefore, I did not have to study as much as I had the first year.

There were two main reasons the Lord asked me to tackle this task, aside from teaching the students the Word. One was to get first-hand experience about how much could be accomplished through the grace of God if life is taken one day at a time. The other was for me to get experience teaching that often. I now teach very often as Dave and I travel and teach plus do our "Life In The Word" meetings at home. God is good, and His ways are perfect.

The other area along these lines that gets people in a lot of trouble is regrets – living in the regrets of yesterday. We all make mistakes. Yes, I said, "We all make mistakes!" Even those people who you think never do anything wrong make mistakes. The Bible says we all have our own little load of oppressive faults. (Gal. 6:5.) We all do and say things we wish we would not have done or said. Once a thing is done, it is done.

I have learned that rather than lose my peace over something that I have done but cannot do anything about now, I should just trust God to make it work out all right. He has that capability you know. He can clean up our mistakes.

Sometimes I say something I wish I would not have said. Instead of worrying about whether or not I offended someone or made them mad, I ask the Lord to let them know my heart was right, even though I put my foot in my mouth. I trust Him to work in their heart and give me favor. That way I do not have to spend several days worrying, then cringe when I see them.

We fall into the trap of regretting many things. Dave and I eat out a lot because we are so busy. Occasionally, we eat someplace where the food is bad or the service is bad. We would find ourselves leaving, then regretting for hours afterward that we had gone there. The Lord showed us that even regrets over a bad choice of restaurants will steal our peace.

Remember, to enjoy peace, stop trying to do something about something you cannot do anything about. Once you have patronized a place of business and paid your bill, regrets will not change what happened.

Now we turn situations like that around and let them work for our good. Now we say, "Just think of all the people who are going to go there and be dissatisfied. Aren't we blessed! We have already found out it is not the place to go. We will never have to waste our time and money there again."

I have a plaque on my wall that reads something like this: If you try to live in the past, life will be hard. Jesus did not say He is the great "I Was." If you try to live in the future, life will be hard. Jesus did not say He is the great "I Will Be." If you take each day as it comes, life will work out all right. Jesus said, "I Am" (John 8:58). He is always with you in each situation that is at hand. Just remember to trust Him for enough grace for today.

Prayer Brings Peace

8

....

Prayer Brings Peace

Philippians 4:6 says:

"Be careful for nothing" (have no anxiety); "but in every thing by prayer and supplication with thanksgiving let your requests be made known unto God.

"And the peace of God, which passeth all understanding, shall keep your hearts and minds through Christ Jesus."

The peace that passes understanding is a great thing to experience. When, according to all the circumstances, you should be upset, in a panic, in turmoil and worried, yet you have peace that is unexplainable, it is a wonderful experience. The world is starving for this kind of peace. You cannot buy it; it is not for sale. It is a free gift from Jesus. It is yours when you accept Him as your Lord and Savior and learn to operate in His principles.

The prayer of commitment is a powerful prayer that moves your burden from you onto Jesus. First Peter 5:7 says, "Casting all your care upon him; for he careth for you." The *Amplified Bible* translation of 1 Peter 5:7 says:

"Casting the whole of your care [all your anxieties, all your worries, all your concerns, once and for all] on Him, for He cares for you affectionately and cares about you watchfully."

What a privilege! Many Christians never use this great benefit even though it belongs to them.

Are you enjoying the peace that results when you cast all your care on Him? The word *cast* means to pitch or throw vehemently. The sooner you do this the better. You do this through prayer. Commit your problems to His loving care. Do this as soon as the Holy Spirit makes you aware that you are worrying or that you have lost your peace.

The devil wants you to worry. First Peter 5:9 (AMP) says to "withstand" the devil "against his onset" – that means at the beginning of the attack, right away. Do not wait until he has had an opportunity to work you over for several days. The longer you wait to resist, the stronger the devil's hold on you will become. Then it is harder to break free. As soon as you realize you are worrying, refuse to worry. Cast the care of the situation on God. *Change your thinking pattern.*

When I was first learning this principle of "casting my care" and "not worrying," I knew my thinking was wrong. I would spend all day casting down imaginations, and they would come right back. I remember being very frustrated about the whole thing. I said to the Lord, "How can a person just not think about something?" You see, in order to not worry, you must not think about the problem. When you do need to think about it to make decisions, you will have to think positively about it and not negatively. You can be realistic about your problem and not be negative.

I still vividly remember what Jesus said to me when I asked, "How can I just not think about this problem?" He said, "It's very simple, Joyce. Just think about something else." You see, you cannot think about the problem if you think about something that is not a problem.

Philippians 4:6 says to not worry but pray instead. Verse 7 promises that if you do verse 6, you will have the peace that passes understanding. Verse 8 (AMP) says:

"For the rest, brethren, whatever is true, whatever is worthy of reverence and is honorable and seemly, whatever is just, whatever is pure, whatever is lovely and lovable, whatever is kind and winsome and gracious, if there is any virtue and excellence, if there is anything worthy of praise, think on...these things...."

Now I pray that God will give you grace, which is the power of the Holy Spirit, to put these principles into practice in your life so that you might enjoy the blessedness of a peaceful life. I also pray that the Father might have free recourse to use you to His honor and glory.

Experience A New Life

If you have never invited Jesus to be your Lord and Savior, I invite you to do so now. You can pray this prayer, and if you are really sincere about it, you will experience a new life in Christ.

Father God, I believe Jesus Christ is Your Son, the Savior of the world. I believe He died on the cross for me, and He bore all of my sins. He paid the price for my sins. He took the punishment I deserved. I believe Jesus was resurrected from the dead and is now seated at Your right hand. I need You, Jesus. Forgive my sins, save me, come to live inside me. I want to be born again.

Now believe Jesus is living in your heart. You are forgiven and made righteous, and when Jesus comes, you will go to heaven.

Find a good church that is teaching God's Word and begin to grow in Christ.

Nothing will change in your life without knowledge of God's Word. John 8:31,32 AMP says, "If you abide in My word...you are truly My disciples. And you will know the Truth, and the Truth will set you free."

Write and let me know you have accepted Jesus and ask for a free booklet on how to begin your new life in Christ.

All of the staff at "Life In The Word" love you. We pray you have been blessed by this book on peace.

Beloved,

John 8:31,32 AMP says, "If you abide in My word...you are truly My disciples. And you will know the Truth, and the Truth will set you free."

I exhort you to take hold of God's Word, plant it deep in your heart and, according to 2 Corinthians 3:18, as you look into the Word, you will be transformed into the image of Jesus Christ.

With Love,
Joyce

About the Author

Joyce Meyer has been teaching the Word of God since 1976 and in full-time ministry since 1980. As an associate pastor at Life Christian Center in St. Louis, Missouri, she developed, coordinated and taught a weekly meeting known as "Life In The Word." After more than five years, the Lord brought it to a conclusion, directing her to establish her own ministry and call it "Life In The Word, Inc."

Joyce's "Life In The Word" radio broadcast is heard on over 250 stations nationwide. Joyce's 30-minute "Life In The Word With Joyce Meyer" television program was released in 1993 and is broadcast throughout the United States and several foreign countries. Her teaching tapes are enjoyed internationally. She travels extensively conducting Life In The Word conferences, as well as speaking in local churches.

Joyce and her husband, Dave, business administrator at Life In The Word, have been married for 31 years and are the parents of four children. Three are married, and their youngest son resides with them in Fenton, Missouri, a St. Louis suburb.

Joyce believes the call on her life is to establish believers in God's Word. She says, "Jesus died to set the captives free, and far too many Christians have little or no victory in their daily lives." Finding herself in the same situation many years ago, and having found freedom to live in victory through applying God's Word, Joyce goes equipped to set captives free and to exchange *ashes for beauty*.

Joyce has taught on emotional healing and related subjects in meetings all over the country, helping multiplied thousands. She has recorded over 170 different audio cassette albums and is the author of 27 books to help the Body of Christ on various topics.

Her "Emotional Healing Package" contains over 23 hours of teaching on the subject. Albums included in this package are: "Confidence"; "Beauty for Ashes" (includes a syllabus); "Managing Your Emotions"; "Bitterness, Resentment, and Unforgiveness"; "Root of Rejection"; and a 90-minute Scripture/music tape entitled, "Healing the Brokenhearted."

Joyce's "Mind Package" features five different audio tape series on the subject of the mind. They include: "Mental Strongholds and Mindsets"; "Wilderness Mentality"; "The Mind of the Flesh"; "The Wandering, Wondering Mind"; and "Mind, Mouth, Moods & Attitudes." The package also contains Joyce's powerful 260-page book, *Battlefield of the Mind*. On the subject of love she has two tape series entitled, "Love Is..." and "Love: The Ultimate Power."

Write to Joyce Meyer's office for a resource catalog and further information on how to obtain the tapes you need to bring total healing to your life.

To contact the author write:

Joyce Meyer
Life In The Word, Inc.
P. O. Box 655
Fenton, Missouri 63026
or call:
(314) 349-0303

*Please include your testimony
or help received from this
book when you write.
Your prayer requests are welcome.*

In Canada, please write:
Joyce Meyer Ministries Canada, Inc.
P. O. Box 2995
London, Ontario N6A 4H9

In Australia, please write:
Joyce Meyer Ministries-Australia
Locked Bag 77
Mansfield Delivery Centre
Queensland 4122
or call:
(07) 3349 1200

Books by Joyce Meyer

Life in the Word Devotional

Be Anxious for Nothing—
The Art of Casting Your Cares
and Resting in God

The *Help Me!* Series:
I'm Stressed!
I'm Insecure!
I'm Discouraged!
I'm Depressed!
I'm Worried!
I'm Afraid!

Don't Dread —
Overcoming the Spirit of Dread
With the Supernatural Power of God

Managing Your Emotions
Instead of Your Emotions Managing You

Life in the Word

Healing the Brokenhearted

"Me and My Big Mouth!"

Prepare To Prosper

Do It! Afraid

Expect a Move of God in Your
Life...Suddenly

Enjoying Where You Are On the Way
to Where You Are Going

*The Most Important Decision
You'll Ever Make*

When, God, When?

Why, God, Why?

The Word, The Name, The Blood

Battlefield of the Mind

Tell Them I Love Them

Peace

The Root of Rejection

Beauty for Ashes

If Not for the Grace of God

By Dave Meyer
Nuggets of Life

Available from your local bookstore.

Harrison House
Tulsa, Oklahoma 74153

The Harrison House Vision

Proclaiming the truth and the power
Of the Gospel of Jesus Christ
With excellence;

Challenging Christians to
Live victoriously,
Grow spiritually,
Know God intimately.